WHEN
LIONS
TALK

The Language of Kings

LIONEL J. TRAYLOR

GWW
PUBLISHING CO.

When Lions Talk
Copyright © 2018 by Lionel J. Traylor.

Published by :
Greater Working Women Publishing Co., LLC
www.gwwpublishing.com

ISBN: 978-1-948829-15-1

10 9 8 7 6 5 4 3 2 1

Dedication

I would like to give thanks to God first and foremost for every blessing, for strength, and for wisdom. To my beautiful wife, Lashawn, thank you for loving me consistently. I love you more! To my children, Nisha, T.J., Keya, Tank, Nue, Slim, LeBee, and Zoe! You're my heartbeat! Your Father loves you all! To my Grandmother, Gracie Lyman, for all of her love, support, and direction. Thank you! To my mother, Lucinda Davis! I love you, mom. You're my Queen! We made it! To my father, "The Original" Lionel Johnson. I love you, dad. Thank you for being "A Man" and always being present. To all my siblings, Shedric, Ebony, Calvin, David, Quentin, Liondra, Thomas, James, Paul, and Patricia. Big brother loves you all. To my Epicenter Church Family, thank you for your trust, love, and loyalty. I love you! Every one of you.

Lastly, to my paternal grandmother, Earlene Hall Johnson! I love you, and I miss you. I thank you for always making me feel special.

Special Acknowledgements

To My Wife, Lashawn Traylor, Dr. C.J. Rhodes, Minister Felix Anderson, and Minister Casandra Ware for helping me organize and getting this work accomplished. Thanks for believing in me.

TABLE OF CONTENTS

FOREWORD   6

INTRODUCTION   8

CHAPTER 1: THE LION'S MIND   10

CHAPTER 2: THE LION'S HEART   18

CHAPTER 3: THE LION'S SPIRIT   28

CHAPTER 4: THE LION'S BODY   36

CHAPTER 5: THE LION'S FAMILY   44

CHAPTER 6: A LION'S RESOURCES   50

CHAPTER 7: A LION'S VISION   58

CHAPTER 8: THE LION'S LEGACY   66

LION KEYS   73

ABOUT THE AUTHOR   87

FOREWORD
Even the lion, the king of the forest,
protects himself against flies. — Ghanaian proverb

Lions are majestic beasts, the monarchs of the jungle. A male lion's mane embraces his face like beams around the sun; his roar strikes fear in the bravest soul. And even the king of beasts protects himself against flies, so the Ghanaian proverb goes. The majestic lion, who is at the top of the food chain, dares not risk being the landing station for pesky insects only smaller than his nostril.

Men would do well to read Lionel's excellent book as the wisdom it contains helps us to shoo away the spiritual, emotional, and mental flies that so easily best us. Bishop Traylor has been a friend and brother for almost ten years, and I have watched him live out the lessons of this book. His testimony is riveting; his "right now" is full of favor. I believe this is because he like his name implies, possesses both the strength and the discernment of a lion. Lions aren't just strong and ferocious, you know. They are thoughtful, clever, pensive. I have witnessed my friend think and pray his way out of struggle and then turn around and help a young cub avoid the dangers he overcame.

Lion Talk is sound advice from an older lion to younger ones that help them be all that God created them to be. Be man enough to read every chapter slowly, digest each sentence, and prayerfully apply the words to your situation. We may be kings, but we don't know how to walk in kingship and to bypass dangers without seeing another king model kingdom royalty before us. Bishop Lionel Traylor has done that in the concrete jungles of New Orleans and Jackson, MS. Now, with this book, he shares excellent knowledge that could save your ministry, your marriage, even your life.

Dr. CJ Rhodes
Pastor, Mt. Helm Baptist Church
Author, 7 Leadership Principles for Service and Success

INTRODUCTION

As far back as I can remember, I have always had a fascination with "Big Cats". Maybe it started with a picture of a "Black Panther" on my aunt Patricia's bedroom wall in the 1980s. I found myself moved by it. But my greater connection has come to the one in which my name is rooted. He is known as the "King of the Jungle". The standard by which all other beasts that walk the earth are judged. But, he is not always the largest, nor the strongest, nor the fastest among them. Yet, he is considered the "King of Beasts". His image has been associated with royalty and greatness for thousands of years in art and philosophy. To wear his carcass is regarded as a symbol of strength. To have his head as a trophy is of great value to those who would hunt for him, even at the hazard of their own lives. Why, you ask? Because it means the "Mighty" has fallen prey to the hands of the ones who are adorned by his mane. They have successfully silenced his roar. Yes, he is mighty. His name has declared his position. He is the LION! The word lion is attributed to "kingliness" or 'grandeur'. The lion's name speaks to his place in the world, and with the name and position comes the expectation; some realistic, some not. His feats are often embellished, as in fork lore, because who he really is as "King" is often shrouded in mystery or misunderstood. We make our judgments and critiques of him through the eyes of filmmakers and the stories told by zookeepers and hunters. Outsiders! Yes, they have a story, but do they really understand what it means to be a LION? To be a King? To be responsible for all under your domain. How could they unless they understood the language of LIONS? How could anyone know what it takes to be a King unless you spoke to a King and he revealed to you "The Secrets of Kingdom". To understand Kings, you must speak the Language of Kings. To understand lions, you must speak with LIONS. Have you ever wondered what it sounds like "When Lions Talk"? In my love of the lion and learning to understand him, I began to really understand myself. Not just merely in my name, 'LION-el", but in my position as a KING. Yes, I did not stutter. As one having been born to one day assume "Rule and Responsibility" for so much that would be placed under my hand. I would be asked to provide, protect, guide, and multiply, all while being challenged by those who wanted or disrespected my position and hunted by those who saw more value in me to them as dead. Was it just me? But the further I searched, I saw an assignment against The Kings of the Earth, "MEN"! Yes, Men! Created by God, "BORN TO RULE". I wrote this book to share secrets with EVERY LION! Young lions and old lions, in every field in which you dwell. It is my hope to impart wisdom, knowledge, and experience in these few paragraphs that will impact you for a lifetime; to speak as a King, the language of Kings, and to speak as a "Man" the conversations "Men" must have in these times.

Let's Talk Lions,
Lionel J. Traylor

CHAPTER ONE

A LION'S MIND

Emotional stability is vital for your promotion's sustainability. Get control of your mind and bring your emotions into subjection.

W hen considering this concept of "When Lions Talk: The Language of Kings", the idea is to show the comparisons and parallels between "The King of the Jungle", The lion, and whom I believe to be "The King of the Earth", The Man. But not merely to reveal the similarities, but to understand the why, who, and what of "this" King. To do so, we must investigate the core, character, complexities, and communication code of the one who is born to be a King. To understand language, one must also understand the thinking of the one articulating. For whether it be verbal, written, or sign, language is an expression of the mind. Language can also be influenced by culture, and culture inspires the soul. Therefore, to truly understand the language of Kings, you must understand the Mind of Kings.

As I began to write this book, I noticed there were similar titles and subject matter already in publication. Many had the exact same content. My initial thought was that surely this topic had been exhausted, and there is nothing new I could add to it. But in my research, I noticed most were surface deep in the information they offered. And I found that none made the comparison that I will make in this book. For instance, let's take into consideration this topic, "The Lion's Mind." Several books on a lion's attitude all say this in some form of fashion... "He is Bold, He is Hungry, He is Aggressive, He is Fearless, and He is Territorial.

He is The LION!! Hear me, ROAR!!" ***smirkishly grinning*** And though all those are attributes of The King of Beast, and at times can be seen of him. It's not him in totality. In fact, I would like to submit, that like everything else in life, that the lion goes through stages of evolution. He goes through stages to become what he was born to be, a King. He will learn along the way how to become a Lion King. He will be taught how to brave the elements of the open prairie. Becoming sensitive to his environment, as to anticipate the attack, how to survive and to prosper knowing you're surrounded by enemies who want nothing more than your place and position. And he must understand that though he is a warrior, he must not be led by his aggression. For anger will blind him and make him vulnerable and more susceptible to his enemies. He must learn that though he is hungry, not to be driven or motivated by hunger alone. For appetite undisciplined will allow him to fall into traps or to bite off more than he can chew. He must be observant when hunting, remembering he himself is being hunted. And one of the most powerful things he possesses, "The Lion's Roar", should only be raised when absolutely necessary.

When I really look at the lion, he shows me why he is King. It's not in his size, his strength, his beauty, or any other physical ability alone. But it is in the thinking of the lion where he has learned these valuable lessons, finding the wisdom to rule. And we, especially as men, must find this wisdom also. For in similar fashion, God made man in his own image and after his own "likeness" and gave him

Dominion and Authority over the earth. God created man as King of the World. And though now, every man is born to rule, he must evolve to become a King. As the lion, men are encouraged to be "Bold as a Lion". To be a man of success, we encourage men to be Hungry! Yes, YOU got to be HUNGRY, Lebron!! (in my Kobe Bryant Voice!) Men are taught to be FEARLESS!! And most of us are territorial. However, though all of those are needed attributes of a man, without "kingly wisdom", this type of man will be a danger to his environment, to all under his dominion, and an even greater danger unto himself.

So, I submit to you that "The Lion's Mind" is diverse. It is NOT a one-size-fits-all. It is a mind that is growing, shifting, evolving, teaching, and teachable. It is the mind of a young lion full of promise and inexperience, to the mind of a matured lion seeking to expand his territory, to an aged lion full of wisdom from words, wars, and wounds. The mind of the lion is the thinking of a young man, housing potential yet needing cultivation. It is the thinking of the matured middle-aged man, who is considering where he is in life, overlooking his accomplishments and failures, contemplating his next move, to the thinking of an aged man, with a head and face full of grey, who has more years behind him than in front of him. He has seen the changes in his environment, and he wonders what he has left that he can offer. His physical ability is abating him. He has fought many wars, buried loved ones, seen bold fools, led by unbridled hunger and aggression, fall prey, and have played the fool himself, but by God's grace, he is still here. The old man knows a fool tells all his heart, so he only speaks now where he can see a wise investment. No, the old lion doesn't roar as much as he used to, but when he does… all under his dominion are familiar with his voice. It is the language of a King in full expression.

Have you ever wondered what it sounds like when Lions Talk?

Reflection and Accountability of
A Lion's Mind

The mind is like a sponge soaking up whatever you put into it. Consider if you are not feeding it spiritual food, then what source are you allowing to feed your mind? What is frequently running through your mind? Do you find it difficult to express your thoughts verbally to others?

A LION PRAYS FOR HIS MIND

Dear Father, I know, as a man, you created me to be the head and to have dominion. I pray for discipline and growth in the areas of my thought life where there's weakness and immaturity. I acknowledge that I don't always think things through as I should, and as a result, I often find myself running to you for a way out of the messes I create. Father, strengthen my mind toward your will, your way, and your word! Help me to slow down and carefully consider how my actions affect not only me but my family and others connected to me. Help me not to run out of your presence so quickly, but sit and listen for your instructions and input. Bring me to a place where I am accountable and purposeful about what I allow in my mind. Set a guard over my mind so that I may be sober and focused as I navigate each day. As the seasons of my life change, allow my mind and perspective to grow, seeing it not through the eyes of disappointment and regret, but as an opportunity to seek you more. In Jesus' Name, Amen.

You're open to threats when you walk in fear. The threat wouldn't make you afraid if fear wasn't present in your heart! The only way to beat fear is to expose it to the light! The threat of losing a job, a house, a business, a spouse, a position, control, your mind, relationships, friendships, a status, a platform, or being alone will only manifest if you let it take root and residence in your mind.

~

Lion Keys

CHAPTER TWO

A LION'S HEART

POWER exposes CHARACTER, and PRESSURE reveals the HEART.

The lion's mentality and exterior are often the focus of attention when describing his character and depicting his image. A symbol of physical strength and mental aggression is often all we come to know of "The King of Beast". And at times, it is all we come to expect of him. In fact, anything outside of physical strength and mental aggression may be perceived as weakness and fear. Especially in the minds of those who have only these two isolated expectations of the lion. In other words, anything less than physical strength and mental aggression makes for one to be "Less Than a Lion". Can I say that I agree? I agree there is a "presence" and a mentality that the lion must possess to be respected in his environment and his place of habitation. If perceived to be weak, a lion's entire rule can be undermined, and his throne will be overthrown. The lion must find the perfect balance of not leading simply "Head Strong" and not relying on "physical intimidation" and "fear" as a means to rule. It is noteworthy to remember that the successful lion must not lead with all head and no heart.

Men are often perceived in the same manner or in the same light. Men are perceived to be mentally more aggressive than his female counterpart. Headstrong is what we as men love to call ourselves when we are overly aggressive. But the term "Pig-headed" is what the women in your life will at times call you when you are "too assertive" or "too aggressive". Think about it, how many times did your mom say you were a "Hard Headed" young man or bullheaded? Have you ever been guilty of being called a "stubborn" old man? If so, then how often were you called this?

The aggression of the lion must be balanced through certain levels of maturity and sensitivity. Yes, I said it. Men must learn to have a healthy balance of sensitivity, and it should not be perceived as weakness. I would dare to say that "Great Men" who have learned to be "Great Leaders" did so by following after their hearts and not a model of "Ruthless Aggression". They were guided by their passions and not by peoples' perceptions. The lion's heart possesses a "Love Language" that is not always clearly understood, but always in expression, and always listens. Love is clearly needed and revealed in every aspect of his life. All men need love and have the need to be loved and have the need to express their love and express their need to be loved. How men express love is different from women. We all know this. At least we should know. Well, now you know. But also, how men express love and the love they need is different based on their place in life. No man is an island. No man wants to be alone. In fact, God said, "It is not good for man to be alone." I believe crimes committed by what the media and criminal analysts have dubbed a "Lone Wolf" is the catastrophe and emotional collapse of a "Lonely Lion". Lions are not meant to be alone. But struggle with saying they are in need of love because they feel it's out of character. The strong, bold, aggressive lion doesn't want to seem weak by saying... "I need to be needed." But Lions are not supposed to be LONERS.

Take into consideration the social construct of lions. Lions are very communal. They migrate together in prides. Lions are typically very, very family-centered and oriented. It's not often that you will see a lion alone, maybe in a battle or a hunt, or maybe leading danger away from the rest of the pride. The false narrative of lions is they do not make themselves vulnerable. But the truth is, every true King will find something worth living for and something worth dying for. The lion's heart is his place of vulnerability. Because he needs to be needed, and though he doesn't wear it on his exterior frame, and you can't see it when he exudes his kingly physical strength. But to those who understand the language of Kings, they understand the heart of the lion is the seat of his vulnerability.

Love Language of Lions

The young lion is often led by his emotions while learning how to walk in wisdom. His curiosity fueled with desire and the need for community, companionship, and affirmation are all driving his aggression. He needs the village for life experiences and the challenges of those within and without to help him to grow in knowledge and strength. He will look for a young love to build him up and to provide for. This is for self-affirmation, to become a young King. He needs to hear her speak of him and his accomplishments with regularity, or he may emotionally detach. It is a crime of his youthful male ego, but it must be fed. For a young lion needs plenty of attention. He may not express it because his young pride will not allow him to be vulnerable or transparent at the moment. But over time, this young lion will learn how to express the Language of Love with more sensitivity, transparency, and vulnerability.

The truth is, it is never easy for a man to leave himself vulnerable, moreover a young man. Though he has a need to be accepted by his equals, celebrated by his companion, and affirmed by his elders, young men are not always good at expressing themselves vocally; especially if there was no older man to teach him how to express himself as a man, not being led only by aggression or relying on physical intimidation. Without the voice of a wise sage, the young man fears the perception of others that his needs are a weakness. It will require patience and understanding to help this young King find a balance.

The mature lion's heart has hopefully transitioned into a place of understanding himself, his Pride, his surroundings, and his role as well as his responsibilities. This lion has come into his reign, and with every passing season, he is establishing himself and operating in his dominion. To me, this is a man between the ages of 30 and 50. He has survived the lust of youth and the youthful mistakes of his late teens and his twenties. Now his moves are more certain, surer, and more calculated. He is leading while still learning. He wants to be established now, and as time moves on, he will desire expansion. For it is a King's nature to conquer and expand territory. It is a King's nature to want his name on all that belongs to him. And in this stage, he still possesses mental aggression and boldness but should possess more knowledge and wisdom about ruling.

As his desires, vision, and worldview change, so will his emotional needs. I believe I heard Bishop TD Jakes say once, "A man doesn't need at 40, what he once wanted at 20." And I wholeheartedly concur. As the young lion, love was about finding self-affirmation. Someone who built him up. So, the question is, "What does he need now?" We would hope that this mature lion has learned the art of expression through verbal dialogue, so those who are under his dominion can respond properly to the King's petitions. But the truth is if the mature lion never learned how to express himself as a young lion, the level of communication may be worse. Why worse? Because years of assuming and trying to "figure" out the language of the King may have allowed for cohabitation, but the heart of the King she may not hold. Yet, she assumes she does. The man he once was may not any longer exist. Therefore, the man she fell in love with may no longer exist either. Why can't he just explain to her what it is he needs? The scary truth is every man needs a man to teach them the manners of Kings.

To teach him how to be transparent and vulnerable, especially while going through changes, including emotional changes.

Younger men, who have not been blessed with the opportunity to learn from a man of wisdom, typically speak all their heart, often without a filter. Being led by aggression, emotions, and a keep it real philosophy. They will release words that wound and can do, at times, irreversible damage. I have seen this also in men who were raised solely by women. This is actually unbecoming of a King. A King cannot at any time speak all his heart without considering his audience and the ramifications of what he may say. Therefore, a man must have a man in his life to impart in him the wisdom to express himself—especially when going through life's transitions.

The mature lion must be vulnerable and transparent with those he will entrust with what he has established and desires to expand, beginning with his lioness. He must be able to convey to her all his heart., all his fears, and all his needs. Her ability to compliment him on this level is why he will give her all his heart. She must be able to hear him and respond accordingly in order to maintain his trust. It is in this season of life where friends will be few, and trust is rare. The one who holds his heart has his ear. He is susceptible to her. At this place, he doesn't need a foolish woman, given to everything but his assignment. His heart he will give, not to the one who builds him up through words, but the one who will build with him through work. She must be bold, strong, and offer knowledge in times of decision making, for she will be a place of strength in his times of weakness and uncertainty. Truth be told, she will have to know her man, her King, her lion so well that she knows what he needs, even without him saying it. For in moments of weakness, men typically won't speak. Kings are instructed not to show weakness. So, though his exterior exemplifies power and might, every man looks for a woman to protect his heart and cover his weakness.

The aged lion has now become set in his ways. He may be very aggressive, snappy, and grumpy. Or very easy, slow-moving, and quiet. However, though his exterior may have changed drastically, his heart has not. In fact, the old lion seems to be more vulnerable than ever the older he gets. I have witnessed some of the sternest preachers to ever mount a pulpit, some of the most hardened military men and some of the shrewdest businessmen, all show their soft spot when it came to their wives, their children, parents, or siblings. Oh, they were warriors. Some had fought wars with no fears and no tears. But when their wives took ill, they were broken. I watched preachers who never smiled as they ministered drool all over themselves with laughter when grandbabies entered the room. The lion's heart makes him very vulnerable in his old age. But it is still what helps him to not lead with all head and no heart. While aging, wisdom should eventually surpass aggression. Love will lead where boldness was once required.

The Fight is there, but peace is preferred, as to enjoy the fruit of his reign, legacy, and prosperity. And those that know the language of the King can see past the old man's exterior, and his grumblings, and hear his heart. A man will give his entire life to simply be loved and needed by those he loves and needs.

Reflection and Accountability of
A Lion's Heart

Walls are erected for two reasons; to keep things out or keep things in. When it comes to your heart lion, what walls have you erected around yours? What or who are you keeping out? What vulnerabilities are you keeping in that need to be exposed for healing to occur?

A LION PRAYS FOR HIS HEART

Dear Father, please create in me a pure, clean heart. Grant me the ability to love unconditionally as you do. Help me to identify threats to my love walk. Help me to be transparent and honest with those I love. Father teach me how to properly communicate the issues of my heart to those I love and those who love me. Teach me how to teach others how to love me sufficiently, without lack or limit. Endow me the resolve to return that love. Give me the capacity to identify and receive true love, knowing its difference from false manipulation that perverts and kills. Remove all blockage and hindrances from my heart. In Jesus' Name, Amen.

Stop letting people walk in and out of
your life at their leisure—especially the
disrespectful and the dishonorable.
Access to your life should be placed at a
high value. Close the door and change
the locks to your heart.

~

Lion Keys

CHAPTER THREE

A LION'S SPIRIT

Everyone wants to make leadership decisions.
Very few are willing to make leadership sacrifices.

T he mind and soul are often interchangeable terms as well as the terms soul and spirit. For the sake of this discussion, where we have investigated the soul of the King (Heart and Mind), I want to delve into the spirit of the King as well. When we say "The Lion's Spirit" or "The Spirit of a Lion", what do we actually mean? In my own perspective, it is what's "instinctive" and what is naturally innate, and an internal part of the lion himself. The lion's spirit is who he is, long before he understands who he is or knows what he shall become. When I think of the word "spirit" and its usage here, the word "influence" comes to mind. There are certain displays and demonstrations in which separate the lion from other beasts of the field and jungle. And he will begin to demonstrate this from his spirit instinctively, long before he can cultivate his abilities consciously.

Why is this important to understand? Because long before the mind can be trained to think a certain way, or the heart taught what to embrace or cast away, the spirit of the lion is open to the influences around him. He will begin to move "instinctively" in the manner and mentality in which he was born. "Probing and Pondering" in and at his surroundings to satisfy his insatiable curiosity to know, understand and figure out his place in the world in which he lives.

In other words, when the lion is born, the spirit is active before the mind and heart can figure things out. The spirit is in operation, exploration, and activation but lacks cultivation and understanding. So, the spirit of the King has been opened to influences since his birth and will continue to be open to influences until death. For "Spirit" is both LIFE and INFLUENCE. For wherever there is a spirit, there is life.

And wherever there is life, there are influences. Now, one of the most dangerous places for a potential King to be is among those who are threatened by his potential. They will seek to take his life. But, if they cannot take his life, they will, in turn, try to "break his spirit". One of the most dangerous places for a reigning King to be is surrounded by negative and unwise counsel. Especially influences that will pervert and destroy his spirit or manipulate him through deception to control the spirit of the King. The lion at all levels must be careful what he allows to influence his potential, cultivation, understanding, and decision making. Whatever influences the "spirit" influences the mind and heart, controls the body, and rules the kingdom.

As MEN, we are so much more than physical strength and aggression. We are "Spirit Beings"! And long before we were able to articulate words to sentences, sentences to paragraphs, and paragraphs to chapters of great literary works, we were great already in spirit, who we were to become. There is a part of the Man, the King of the World, that is ageless and carries in him the Image and Likeness of The King. And from the day that a man breathed in life, he became a "living spirit". Meaning the body is alive because of the spirit. So, it is the spirit that gives life. Therefore, if I want to manipulate the man, I must manipulate his spirit. For the spirit influences or gives life to the man.

Let me give a quick example:

From the day of a man's birth, he desires to be able "to do more. I believe because he is driven by the spirit of life instinctively. As a baby, he will one day roll off his back, onto his belly with eyes wide open, looking to understand his surroundings. He maneuvers on his belly and from his belly to his knees to crawl in an attempt "to become more" self-mobile. He crawls and pulls himself up, driven to "become more" than what and where he was yesterday. This is a sign of life. Growth and Movement! Even without a complete understanding of who or what he is, he is moving. Now, he depends on those in his "life" to supply the things he needs to sustain life until the day comes that he can sustain his life on his own. It is in those years where he is most dependable on others, where he is also very impressionable by the influences surrounding him."

This is where I see a MAN can be robbed of his masculinity, his manly responsibilities, detoured from his destiny, and lose his sense of spirituality. How, you might ask? It is very simple yet complex. It is all simply because those who do not understand the "Language of Kings" will discourage him from his instincts instead of properly cultivating them. And as he grows and moves through life, he moves and grows further away from what he was born to be and to do... BORN TO RULE. The spirit of a man, given to a man at birth, is carrying the instructions of the King of Heaven, to be uploaded into the biological hardware of man at the moment life was conceived. Those instructions were... Be Fruitful, Multiply, and to have Dominion.

These instructions are carried into every man in his spirit, from the "Spirit" that created him. Every force, every entity, any energy, spirit or persona that cannot understand, or chooses not to receive "The Language Of The King Of Heaven" will fight "The King Of Earth" from walking in the "spirit" of The Ruler and fulfilling the instructions from God written on his DNA. And that is to "Rule Responsibly." And this is what must drive the lion, not his belly, but his spirit!

Sometimes we can desire success for people more than they desire it for themselves. We can become more invested in their gifts, opportunities, relationships, ministry, health, and family more than they are willing to invest in those areas themselves. You should invest ONLY where you expect and receive a good return. To continue to invest time, resources, counsel, etc., into those types of people is unwise stewardship, and it will only yield you the dividends of frustration in your life while creating a spirit of entitlement and laziness in those who should be working just as hard as you are about their own success. Some people don't want to CHANGE. They just want your CHANGE. Don't Stop Investing... Just find others to invest into.

Reflection and Accountability of A Lion's Spirit

God communicates with us by his Spirit, through his word, in prayer, and in dreams. He's often speaking in subtle ways, but always by his Spirit. Can you think of a time when you couldn't hear God? Was it the result of a spirit disconnection? What was going on in your life at that moment? What steps have you taken since to prevent a repeat?

THE LION'S PRAYS FOR HIS SPIRIT

Dear Father, help me to guard the gates of my spirit! Guard oh God, my eyes, my ears, my heart, and my mind! Guard my spirit from things that will pervert and delay your purpose for my life and my family! Hear my cry, oh Lord, to bring my spirit in alignment with your spirit, from which life flows. Strengthen me to discern the difference between demonic influences and your divine influence. Purify my spirit, that I may hear you clearly when you are releasing instructions, wisdom, warnings, and revelation for my life. Mature me, Lord, that I may walk in the spirit and not after the lusts and desires of my flesh that are intensified when I have neglected my commitment and relationship with you! Forgive me! I want my spirit to be pleasing to you! I want to stay connected to you! In Jesus' Name, Amen.

You don't have any more points to
prove! You don't have to respond!
You don't have to fight!
You don't have to agonize!
Let Go and Live! You don't have any
more points to prove!

~

Lion Keys

CHAPTER FOUR

A LION'S BODY

"Your BODY is only as strong as your core. The stronger your core is, the more you will be able to do with the rest of the BODY!"

S ought after for his head and his coat, by admirers and enemies, the lion's body is a symbol of great prestige, royalty, and kingliness. But the King of The Jungle must take care of his body, not so much for the onlookers, who appreciate the display of strength and beauty of "the lion's body", but for many other pivotal reasons. Several components of communication between lions involve body language, scent, and the lion's roar. That's right, "The Language of Kings" is non-verbal, as well as verbal communication. I would dare to say, more non-verbal than verbal. His physical stature can speak volumes of his mentality, emotional stability, and position in life.

For instance, I have heard it said that a lion that holds his head up when sitting and walks with an erect posture, or to say, "with his chest out", is most likely holding a high position in the tribe. And his "Body Language" is communicating that to other male lions in the tribe and from other tribes that he is in charge of. To the lionesses and young cubs, they recognize his "Body Language" as saying," He is the one in charge." From that point, he is being physically sized up by those who desire his position. The Lion King must be as physically strong as he can be to withstand the multiple challenges that come with being King. He will need endurance to successfully defend his kingdom, his family, and his position. Longevity gives The Lion King an opportunity for more than just a long existence, but greater opportunity for expansion and elevation of his kingdom. But he must age wisely, taking into consideration that any signs of physical weakness to his enemies may cause an uprising or an overthrow of his position.

His body language must be that of strength to all who draw from his strength until the time comes where they are strong enough to stand without him.

There is a difference between walking in arrogance or pride and walking in confidence. As a young man, my father would try and teach me the difference. I would watch my father up close and from afar. His "Body Language" spoke volumes to me as a child, even into my teenage years, as I looked to this "Lion" for everyday guidance and understanding of myself. My father stands about 6 feet tall, and his weight varies at times, but I would think he stays between 165-180 pounds. He has an athletic build, is lean, muscular, and he is very vascular. I remember thinking as a young boy, "look at all those veins in his hands and arms." He walks with his chest out and his head up. He greets friends with a smile and firm handshake and the ladies with a "Hey Ba-by, how ya doin'!", accompanied with a hug or kiss. He speaks with authority in his voice, like a general at a command center or a king when you are summoned into his presence. Where my mother or grandmother would shout my entire government name to gather my attention… "Lionel Joseph Traylor!" My father could gather that and more by only saying my name… "Lionel!" I can hear his voice as I write these words. His voice and stature were unmatched in the house, and in my mind, he had no equivalent in the entire tribe. His hands firm, eyes stern, and voice strong. He would work out routinely, as plastic covered cement weights, in colors of red and blue, sat on the floor near his bedside, on a curl bar. He would drink two or three raw eggs in the mornings before going to work some blue-collar job that demanded his stamina and strength. His body was his tool used to supply goods for the family. His Body was our means for Provision and Protection. I wanted to be STRONG like him. Not just physically strong, but mentally, emotionally, and even spiritually. Because to me, when he walked into the house, his "Body Language" said it's going to be okay the King's home. As I have grown older, I understand his body language more now than ever and can see the changes his body has gone through. His body language is different now, but still confident and strong.

The lion communicates with other lions, his lioness, his cubs, and all under his kingdom through body language. Your scent is speaking. This is true of all of creation and is true of you! In fact, lions use scents to identify each other. Scent is used to identify their cubs. Every tribe has a unique scent. This is how they distinguish one from another. This is how other lions know if your lioness belongs to you. The lioness begins to take on the scent of her lion. Yes, she knows your scent. But, do you know your scent? What is your signature smell? Is it a floral scent? Is it a fresh scent? Or is it woody? Your scent speaks for you.

My father would wear Old Spice and Brute Cologne back in the 1980s. The bathroom and his bedroom smelled like him. When I first tried on cologne… it was his. I was nine or ten years old, smelling like Old Spice and Brute. Soon my younger brothers would follow suit. Eventually, the whole tribe smelled like Old Spice (laughing uncontrollably). The Language being communicated from the King's Body is this is my Tribe, with my scent on them. When I came into my own kingdom, I established my own scent. My fragrance will now fill my bathroom and the bedroom. Our bedroom sheets have the scent of the man of the house… ME. My young sons borrow their father's cologne, and my daughters try and place my scent on their boyfriends. Because the scent is that of the King, and it speaks of his presence.

Then there is the lion's roar. The lion's roar doesn't just require his voice, but his physical strength. The roar of the lion is used to establish order, to announce his presence, his authority, and to communicate to outsiders, "I am still strong enough to fight." But when a lion is defeated, he loses his roar. Often as men, when we feel our bodies are betraying us, we begin to mentally or emotionally feel weak. When we don't feel strong enough, tall enough, young enough, or too old, we can lose our roar. When we don't feel capable, or we feel physically inadequate, our body language says it all, even if we never open our mouths. Typically, men don't speak when they feel defeated or physically inadequate. We lose our roar. Men, we must do our best to take care of our bodies, because lions are speaking with their bodies, The Language of Kings.

Do you know what it looks like When Lions Talk?

Reflection and Accountability of A Lion's Body

In 1 Corinthians 6:19-20, the Bible details that as believers, not only do our bodies not belong to us but God, we are the house (the temple) for the Holy Ghost! Reflecting on that, what are some things that you need to address in your body to ensure that the Holy Ghost always has a home in you?

THE LION PRAYS FOR HIS BODY

Dear Father, I realize my body is the temple, the house for the Holy Ghost, and I acknowledge that at times I have not protected and treated it as such. Lord, I understand that in order for me to fulfill your purpose for my life, in addition to a strong mind, a strong heart, and a strong spirit, my vessel must be submitted and strong as well. Help me to make wiser decisions about what I put in my vessel and what I do with my vessel. Father, I want to be both spiritually and physically strong so that I may protect all that you've given me dominion over, especially family. I pray where there are battle wounds and scars or sickness, that you heal and restore me. Forgive me where I have been neglectful concerning my temple, not realizing that I have opened doors for the enemy to attempt to shorten my life, hinder my purpose, and cut me off from my promise! Thank you for revealing it to me. Lord, I need your help in this area. Strengthen me for this course! Fortify my mind that I may walk in victory. In Jesus' Name, Amen.

Body Language can speak Louder at times than words. Pay close attention to those you have at your table. Your success depends upon your ability to discern who to trust with the keys.

~

Lion Keys

CHAPTER FIVE

A LION'S FAMILY

"Your life, business, family, or ministry can change in one moment. Are you prepared?"

My father, to me, is the physical example of old school masculinity. Not a perfect man, but a man sure enough. A man of his time… "When men were men", as the old saying goes. A Hard-working, 40 hours plus a week type of man. And if he lost a job, he was a… "get out there and find a hustle type of man." He would do all the hard, physical, dirty jobs, and blue-collar jobs if it helped pay the bills. He would watch gangster movies, Kung Fu, and Westerns on Saturdays. Sundays were all about Family, and the Lord has always been a part of his conversation with his family. He is the eldest child of 4 siblings, and they were raised by their mother. I don't know all the logistics of why my grandfather wasn't present in their life, but it made my father very protective of his mother and siblings. He would always check on the women in the family, my grandmother and great aunts. Am I saying my father is perfect? No. But he has always been present. And willing to sacrifice himself for his family. Because to my father, family is everything.

I guess that's where I get it from. The old school mentality concerning "a man and his home". That his home is his castle, and his family is royalty. That his woman is his Queen and his seed is royal. To me, the greatest gifts in this life have come in the form of my children. I have been blessed with eight beautiful, creative, intelligent, very strong, and very opinionated children. As a King, I expect my house, my kingdom, to be in subjection to me, but I don't treat them as "subjects", but as "royalty". For it is the heart of a man to give all that's good in this life to his family. There is a passage in the scriptures that says, "It is the Father's great pleasure to give you the Kingdom." My heart echoes those sentiments exactly for my family. I want to give them the best life has to offer.

This is the lion's mentality concerning his family. Though he is the King of the Jungle, he will hazard his life in an attempt to provide for his family. And he takes great pride in doing it himself. He takes great pride in earning the kill, working for it himself, and dragging the carcass of what he has seized and conquered back home. I once asked the question, "Why would a lion attack a beast twice his size to eat?" The answer was simple, "He has a family to feed." Not all men are taking on great loads, attempting great feats, and pushing themselves to the breaking point, trying to prove a point. But some simply may have more responsibility than others. More responsibility than you can see. And just enough may not be enough when you're responsible for the livelihood of The Tribe. There is some young lion forced to presently be a provider, right now at this very moment, simply because there is no King at home. There is a lioness carrying her load alone in all her Queendom because, for whatever reason, there is no King present. And though they may be successful, even to the point of greatness. The Tribe has no "Scent" of a King.

And life becomes that much more difficult without the ability to be identified as belonging to The Tribe of a certain King. Provision and Protection of the family are given by the King. I am certain that this is the responsibility of a man. A responsibility that he prides himself in; to provide for his family. A God-given responsibility etched into the very fabric of a man's DNA, but it must be pulled out of him and cultivated. To be a King means to be responsible for all under your jurisdiction. And a TRUE KING, A TRUE LION… A REAL MAN would not have it any other way.

Reflection and Accountability of
A Lion's Family

As head of the family, people look to you for answers you don't always have, causing you to take a trial and error approach at times. As a son, a father, or as a husband, what would you say your greatest challenge is? If your family graded you, what do you think your grade would be? If you had an opportunity to do over anything, what would it be, and what would you do differently to get a different outcome?

THE LION PRAYS FOR HIS FAMILY

Dear Father, please help me to successfully carry the weight of being a son, a husband, and a father. I realize how crucial my presence and my direction are for the success of my family. Help me to make the necessary sacrifices and walk with wisdom as I steer us forward in your will and ways. Help me to teach my sons how to be men of integrity and accountability, but also men of prayer and sensitivity. Help me to teach my daughters to know their worth and value, to be strong and independent, but also to know what real love is. Help me to love and nurture and affirm and support my wife by giving her what she needs to be all you created her to be. I ask you, Father, when my load gets heavy, strengthen me to endure and that you replenish me in my weak areas. I understand my family is a gift and an extension of me. Open my eyes and heart that I may receive guidance from you when I just can't see my way clear or when I'm frustrated. Keep me humble so that I may apologize when I'm wrong and be quick to forgive offenses. I want my family to make it! I want my family to be happy and successful! Lord, I bring all my fears, all my shortcomings, all my mistakes before you and ask that you lead and guide me, so that I may lead and guide them. In Jesus' Name, Amen.

The truth is some of those who we call "FAMILY" are no more than "FAMILIARS". And because we know them as KIN, we won't acknowledge the poison within. Snakes shed SKIN. Same serpent, different skin. And oftentimes, the spirit shows up in your KIN.

~

Lion Keys

CHAPTER SIX

A LION'S RESOURCES

Never make a partnership with an angry or bitter person. Their wounds will cause them to make emotional and erratic decisions that will hurt you in the long run.

As I looked more into the life of a lion, the more I realized that in his passion for his family and his pride in his position, both were firmly tied to his ability to provide for his kingdom. For both passion and position is empty without provision. Without provision, a Kingdom is simply a dying dynasty, often waiting to turn on itself in cannibalism, as it becomes "survival of the fittest. To maintain his kingdom, his role as King makes him responsible for finding provisions and keeping the tribe safe. The lion, as leader of the tribe, must lead his family to a place where provision is plenteous. Or at least make sure that provision makes it to his tribe. This is where an understanding of resources can determine longevity or merely sustainability, at least until the next opportunity presents itself. A lion's resources can determine the health and well-being of his tribe. His resources can determine the strength of the tribe in numbers and physical ability. A lion's resources determine the way in which the lion rules, and often how others will approach him.

I often hear the phrase, "You know, it is a Jungle out there", referring to the way of the world, that it can be a hard place to maneuver and survive, let alone conquer. Yet, inside of every King, there must be something he has dominion over. Something that he can say, "This... is mine." So, he delves out into the jungle, looking for something to define him. We often set out on passion but end up settling at provision. Why, haven't you heard? "It's a JUNGLE out there?" And because it is, many of us shift our minds from conquering to survival. We just want enough to maintain or sustain what we have. But one thing I know about having just enough, there will come a day where it is not enough. Atmospheres shift, and so do economies. Children grow, and so does the tribe. New mouths will need feeding. New heads and hearts will need protecting. And it's the lion's responsibility to find new resources or multiply the resources he has.

I mentioned earlier in this book that I often wondered about the mental stability of a lion who would chase down a beast as large as him to satisfy his hunger. I said too, like many other onlookers, that this is the definition of the male ego, "Biting off more than they could chew." At the start, I too agreed... But at closer inspection, I come to learn that this is a "King" responsible for the livelihood of his tribe. So, he cannot come home with just enough for him. He must come home with more than enough; enough to feed everyone tonight, tomorrow, and hopefully a many a day after. And then he must eye, attack, bite down and conquer again, something greater than himself, to leave something more for his family. So, he goes to work, and no matter what his occupation is, in the jungle of life, he is "The Lion". He can be a mechanic, a plumber, a preacher, or an artist. In his mind... He is 'The Lion". He can be a waiter, a lawyer, a software programmer or a professional athlete. In his mind, he is in this jungle trying to provide resources, and livelihood, for his tribe. He is "The Lion!" No matter the occupation or work he does, in his mind, it's all the same... It's a jungle out here. How do I come home with more than enough?

In a documentary on "The Secret Lives of Lions," one way these lions were able to continue to have more than enough provision was by working together. Partnerships allowed for the consistent success of large-scale animals. I watched as several lions worked in conjunction to take down a huge elephant. In the beginning, no one attacked the head. They all with one effort, attacked the rear legs of the animal until it was so wounded it had to come down. In the beginning, the elephant tossed to and fro. He was swaying and stepping, using its strength to push one and two of them off his huge frame. But the lions were persistent in their attack and focused on where to attack until finally, the elephant came down. Then one of the lions jumped on his back and went for his head. The elephant finally accepted its demise. The partnership of lions produced a swift and calculated victory. And every lion went home with more than enough provision for the day. I believe every lion needs a "Circle" of lions in which they can work together to do what they could not do alone. How do you eat an elephant? One bite at a time, of course. But does every bite have to be yours? In other words, every bite from a different lion working in concert brought the elephant down swifter and with less individual energy and effort.

As men, we are responsible for our families (tribes). But also, with an understanding of the times, your area, your family needs, and your vision, you may need a partner or partners. In the words of King Solomon, "Two or Better than one and a threefold cord is not easily broken." Sometimes as men, we know it's our responsibility to provide, and we take great pride in it. I know I do. But I honestly can say I have had (and still do have) great partners. I often say, "Every man needs a man." Every man at one point has been a boy. Every teacher, a student. Every preacher, a disciple. Every General, a Soldier. Every Father, a son. In understanding resources, what man are you gleaning from? For every stage of life, you must have someone to prepare you for that stage. And someone to guide you through that stage. Consider the great Lebron James, not the athlete, but the businessman. Basketball is what he does to gain resources... But in his mind, he is just a lion in the jungle. He knows you can have resources today and die of hunger tomorrow. So, to avoid never being broke again, to the best of his ability, he built partnerships with those who understand wealth on levels he had not dreamed of. And these partnerships helped him take down elephants swiftly and with less energy and effort as if he went at it alone. One of the greatest financial minds in the world today, Warren Buffett, is one of James' financial advisors. He pays him well for his time and his financial advice. Some will not see the wisdom in that... but everyone doesn't understand "The Language of Kings." But I hope you do.

Hey Lion... Who's In Your Circle?

Reflection and Accountability of
A Lion's Resources

When we consider the subject of resources, many think they have it all figured out, even though they are living check to check with no provisions laid up beyond a couple of days or more. It's never too late to turn things around. Have you sat down and considered how you can build up your resources so that there's sufficiency for your home and family? Have you passed down practices and knowledge to your wife and children in the event that something happens to you? Have you connected to someone with more wisdom than you in this area so that you may grow and expand?

A LION PRAYS FOR HIS RESOURCES

Dear Father, create in me the ability to be a resource for my family, being a provider of spiritual and natural necessities. Divinely connect me to people and places, not only to benefit me, but for those I cover and have dominion over. Father, I pray for the wisdom and understanding to be a good steward over the resources you have entrusted me with. May the wisdom of Joseph be upon me, that even in times of famine, my family nor I will suffer lack! I pray for insight on ways to duplicate that wisdom, knowledge, and maturity in my children and my children's children. I pray for favor to walk in abundance, having not just enough, but more than enough. I want sustainability! I want overflow! I know it's your will that I will be abundantly blessed in every area of my life. Teach me your ways and principles for provision, Father! Reset my mind and cleanse away all my bad habits in this area.
In Jesus' Name, Amen.

Ask God for wisdom and discipline
concerning your resources.
Use budgeting practices, faith, and
wisdom in your giving, and learn wealth
building principles.

~

Lion Keys

CHAPTER SEVEN

A LION'S VISION

"My purpose drives me! The vision inspires me! God's word is guiding me FORWARD!"

It is virtually impossible to separate the word "Vision" from "Leadership". The two of them go hand in hand. For it is of a truth when the scriptures said, "If the blind lead the blind, they will both fall into a ditch." Blind leadership is limited leadership. It is leadership that can only go as far as it can feel. It is leadership without sight, foresight, insight, oversight, and spiritual sight. Truth be told, the one with the position is honestly NOT the leader... The one with "the vision" is. Question: Are you following a Blind Man? Is the King Blind? How is your sight? As "The King of the Jungle", one of the lion's greatest abilities is his keen sense of vision. It is said that in the daylight, a lion's sight is no different than that of humankind. And in complete darkness, like ours, the lion is also limited.

But, under the nighttime sky, under the moon, and stars, it is said that the lion's Vision is eight times greater than that of man or the average animal under the same circumstances. This is one of the reasons lions do most of their hunting at night. Under the cover of darkness, and with the ability to see in the distant dark, The King conquers and defeats more of his prey at night than in the daylight.

I am convinced that this VISION is a quality that separates Kings from Jesters and the Men from the boys. To the lion, being King is not just what you are able to conquer when the sun is shining, and everyone is looking, and when things seem to be safe. But what will you do when night falls? When darkness is upon your kingdom, and things look scary, and the night creatures are on the prowl, what do you see now? Because as the King, as the leader, as the man, you must have the ability to see in the dark. You must be able to still cast vision in the nighttime. You must find a way to continue to provide, protect and pursue, even under the cloud of darkness that will come to your kingdom from time to time. This is what makes the lion "The Apex Predator"! His ability to perform in the night season.

Sometimes when things are going too well, "The King" in men becomes comfortable. When the sun is shining, we are often at rest, shading under a tree—or perched in a high place enjoying all under our dominion. But in the nighttime, our eyes open wider. Vision becomes larger, as it seems pressure and problems spark our creative genius. It is the challenge of the night that awakens us. We were created to conquer. We were born to rule. The King in man responds to the night, not with his mouth, but with his eyes and with his actions. He becomes quiet, but he is moving. He is moving slowly, but he is contemplating his next move in the night.

When you learn the Language of the King, you will know that when men go quiet that they are not disengaged, but fully engaged. They are thinking. Kings have learned they cannot share their vision with many for several reasons. So, they move in the dark, in silence, casting vision, defeating enemies, providing for their tribe, and conquering territory. Learn to move in silence. It is called casting "Vision" not "Vocals!"

I married when I was very young, 21 years old to be exact. My wife was 18 years old at the time our family was readymade, four children, at the time with one baby girl on the way. I wasn't intimated about our situation, but at the same time, I was not completely cognitive of it either. My understanding at the time of what it would really require maintaining such responsibility was juvenile at best. But I was in love with my wife and in love with my children. I was in love with the dream of having a family of my own, having my own place, being my own man. I was ready for a new life and to walk in the purpose for my life. I had a dream... But I had no vision. The vision came to me in the darkest places of my marriage and ministry. In the still of the nighttime situations of my life, I had to look within myself, and to God in ways I had never looked before, to see things in me and around me that I never knew were there. My vision for my marriage, family, and ministry, became clearer in the night seasons of my life. Oversight is what I was given but was also what I needed. The insight came with my experiences and continued mentorship. Foresight came through the pain of past mistakes, prayer, planning, and a promise to go forward. Spiritual sight is what God reveals to me when it is hidden from me, so I have no fear of the dark places in my life. In fact, I can honestly say for myself, that I believe I perform better with my back up against the wall than having no pressure at all. Pressure and Problems awaken the King in me, and the lion begins to quietly stalk in the nighttime what may have escaped him in the day.

King, you will VALUE your VISION more in the night season than in the sunshine. And those under your leadership will VALUE you as the VISIONARY when you lead them through the night season of their lives protected and provided for.

King, can I ask you a question? How is your vision in the night?

Reflection and Accountability of A Lion's Vision

When we consider what blindness is, it's fair to say that it is the lack of vision or the inability to see. In the natural, one is either born blind, or one can become blind sometimes at their own hands. But vision isn't just sight, it can be a driving force or goal. Can you think of any area in your life that lacks vision? And if you have discovered life's vision, who else knows what your vision is? Who's helping you bring it to pass?

A LION PRAYS FOR HIS VISION

Dear Father, give me divine sight and insight, seeing well in the natural and in the spiritual. Help me to see things as you do. Help me not to be blind in areas that are critical to my success and the success of those I have been given charge and dominion over. Bring to light those things hidden in darkness that may cause me to stumble and fall. Shine light, Father, even on any darkness within me, that I may be delivered and truly be a light unto others. Father, give me clarity concerning my purpose so that the vision I have for my life does not conflict with yours. Teach me how to guard my vision. Enable me to be selective in who I choose to help me bring my life's visions and dreams to pass. I realize now that everyone can't go where I'm going because they can't see where I'm going. Help me to be spiritual, not emotional in these matters, knowing that where there's no vision, those I have charge over will perish.

I acknowledge I am the VISION holder for my tribe. And I acknowledge I don't have all the answers, and sometimes I'm fearful of messing it all up. Thank you, father, that you hear my heart and that in you I find hope and no failure! In Jesus' Name, Amen.

The VISION is speaking to me VERY
LOUDLY. The night has not given my
eyes any sleep but has given me
GREATER INSIGHT! We are Greater
Than Where We Are! We Are Greater
Than What We Are! Mediocrity Is
Unacceptable! Kingdom Excellence Is
Not an Option! Holiness Is Not an
Option! Commitment Is Not an Option!
GLORY IS NOT AN OPTION!

~

Lion Keys

CHAPTER EIGHT

A LION'S LEGACY

Success is a matter of choice, and so is failure.
Choose Life!

A s we considered the lion and his Kingdom and made the comparison to The Man his Kingdom, one thing comes to my mind now... How does it all end for The King? And what shall become of his kingdom? For we have established that a man finds his purpose in those he feels responsible for. Those who are under his dominion are those he feels deep inside of himself that he was created for. Covenants he has made to expand his kingdom, wars he has fought to protect his kingdom, and mammoths he has taken down to provide for his kingdom. All he has ever done was for his tribe and for his kingdom. Every man thinks of the day he moves on to the place where he is no longer able to do those things or when he crosses over to the next life... What shall become of my tribe? What shall my Legacy be?

The word "Legacy" has been simply defined as an amount of money or property left to someone in a will. I do suppose that land and resources can be a part of a legacy. The scripture does tell us that a "good man" leaves an inheritance for his children's children. But I would beg to differ if this is "legacy" in its entirety, for I am one who believes that your true legacy is not what you purchased, but what lives after you. Something that cannot be brought, sold, or exchanged. Something greater than stone monuments and steel buildings.

I watched the transition of power among the lions, as the once youthful, strong and mighty, agile, ferocious, fearless, King of Beasts became older, heavier, slower moving, weaker, and believe it or not, somewhat fearful, depending on the transition. Let's be real here. In the wild, the transition of power is almost never graceful. It's almost always ugly, as The King begins to wonder who in the tribe will take him down for his position and for power over his kingdom. I think some of us have these fears also...

Though often not expressed, we fear what will become of all we worked for. All we built and all we brought. But can I tell you the things are not your legacy? King Solomon says to us in the book of Ecclesiastes that when we die, we can take none of these things with us and asked the question, "Who shall all these things be?" Am I saying we should not build or leave an inheritance of things behind for families? No, I am not saying that. But I am saying your legacy is much bigger than the stuff you possess or things you can purchase. Your legacy is about those you have been given the privilege to have influence over. There are three things you will leave on this earth after this life, even if you never own a business, buy land, or write a book.

Those three things are:
1.   Your Blood
2.   Your Name
3.   Your Influence

These three things are your legacy and how you will be remembered. Your bloodline will remain in the earth as long as you have a seed or family in the earth. Blood speaks of family origin, history, and legacy. If you are privileged to have children (seed) in the earth, then they will continue your life in the earth in the form of legacy. If you never own land, your seed will be your memorial in the earth. Our children are worth the investment. I pray God gives you honorable children that will bring honor to your bloodline.

That next thing is your name. The bible says, "A Good Name is to be chosen over rubies." A good name is a rich legacy. When your name is spoken as a King, what will the consensus be? As a man, we should be concerned about the condition of the name we leave behind more than the money we leave behind. Because when the money is gone, the name remains. Or what good is it to have wealth and riches, but a bad name associated with it? You want to have a name that your loved ones can be proud of long after you have left this life. As a father, grandfather, husband, son, grandson, pastor, I am concerned about my name... because legacy is tied to so many lives. I want to leave my loved ones a good name.

And finally, as an influencer, your greatest legacy is found in those you inspire and what you inspired them to do. It is said a lion's roar can be heard up to 5 miles in the distance from the place he releases his roar. Those who are closes can not only hear him but feel his strength in his roar. The roar will cause different reactions in those that hear it. But to those kingdom connections and those who are of his tribe, they will be inspired. With the strength God gave you to inspire, what are you influencing those in your tribe and kingdom to become? What are you moving them toward? For every inspired person is a part of your legacy. Every young lion that becomes King, because of your example, he is part of your legacy. Every person you push to become better, they are a part of your legacy. They will tell the stories behind the stone monuments, steel buildings, banners, and plaques. They will be the testimonies of "A Good Man" that made sacrifices for his family and inspired others. For "The Legacy of a Good King" is not told in tales of just brick, stone, and steel. But in every life impacted through love, wisdom, and inspiration.

In The Language of Every King is the question...
"How will I be remembered?" The answer is simple...
"King, You Will Be Remembered How You Lived!"

Reflection and Accountability of
A Lion's Legacy

The bible tells us in the first chapter of the book of Genesis that every seed produces after its own kind. Your life is a seed. It will produce. It will duplicate. It will be on full display for others to see, AND it will point directly back to you. What do you want your seed (legacy) to say about you? How can you change what you produce moving forward?

A LION PRAYS FOR HIS LEGACY

Dear Father, help me create a legacy of service and selflessness for those I am responsible for and connected to. Father, you said a good man leaves an inheritance to his children's children. Pour into me what I need to pour into them, that they may not only survive but thrive well beyond me, not just financially but spiritually and mentally. I pray to live a life before them that will bring them no shame even when I am no longer here. I pray that my life inspires and influences others to look to you for all the answers to the questions life surely will present. Teach me how to live a life that encourages others to see themselves as you see them. Teach me, Father, how to be a good example of a provider, a protector, a husband, a father, a friend, a kingdom ambassador... a man after your heart! This Father, is the legacy I want to leave. In Jesus' Name, Amen.

"The most dangerous people to your anointing are your familiars. Because they're so close to you, they don't value you. And when they don't value you, the enemy can use them to destroy you!"

~

Lion Keys

LION LIFE LESSONS

GOVERN YOURSELF ACCORDINGLY

Those that are not teachable are unsuccessful...

"Real Change is never easy, but always accompanies growth. If you're not changing... you're not growing, not expanding, not building, but most importantly, not learning."

~

Lion Keys

"The key to successfully carrying any weight is balance. Get balanced and be successful."

~

Lion Keys

"When in pursuit of happiness, make purpose your pursuit. For without the living in and the fulfillment of purpose, life is meaningless. Therefore, making all happiness temporal and void."

~

Lion Keys

"When you are a DRIVEN person, all distractions in life are speed bumps, not stops. People of PURPOSE are full of PASSION and have only two types of people in their lives; those you roll with and those you roll over!"

~

Lion Keys

"Some wars are not worth the
resources spent to fight them.
Investigate before you Invest. Always
ask yourself, 'Are the spoils of battle
worth engaging this enemy?'"

~

Lion Keys

"Religion tells me what I cannot do!
But 'THE KINGDOM' shows me what
I CAN!"

~

Lion Keys

"A seed of dishonor can cost you a harvest of favor!"

~

Lion Keys

"Emotional instability is a sign of spiritual immaturity. We can make our choices, but we cannot choose our consequences. A secret to stability and happiness in life is not to try to please people but to please God. Herein lies the joy of living."

~

Lion Keys

"Everything that has been fractured and broken may not be worth repairing. For some of us, "brokenness" was the only way God could give you 'wholeness.'"

~

Lion Keys

"Many people can't walk in
gratefulness because they haven't been
through anything or haven't been
through enough! When you've really
been through hell to the point that you
find out God was all you had,
gratefulness will come easy! Lifting
your hands will be easy!"

~

Lion Keys

"What is in us given the proper environment or situation will manifest itself. Adversity will expose our character, temptation our lust, offense our love, and trials our faith."

~

Lion Keys

"One act of PRIDE can cost you the kingdom. BUILD IN HUMILITY."

~

Lion Keys

"When EXCELLENCE becomes an option and not a standard. You will become optional to those who have a standard."

~

Lion Keys

ABOUT THE AUTHOR

Bishop Lionel J. Traylor is the founder of The Epicenter Church, a progressive ministry that serves hundreds of worshipers weekly and is positioned in the heart of Jackson, MS. With an unwavering mandate from God, Lionel J. Traylor's mission has been to establish the kind of ministry that is devoted to restoring communities, serving the impoverished, restoring families, and strengthening individuals within the body of Christ locally, nationally, and worldwide. With over 20 years in ministry and 12 years of pastoring, Bishop Traylor is a renowned and respected spiritual leader, reformer, and trend-setter for change in both the religious and secular arena. His sound teaching, fatherly coaching, and ability to mold leaders is transforming the city of Jackson and the surrounding areas.

Bishop Traylor has preached the Gospel nationwide and has shared platforms with national and international influential speakers and leaders, appearing on both TBN and The Word Network, respectively.

With over two decades of ministry, marriage, and eight wonderful children between them, the Traylors are favored by God and have been positioned for greatness.

www.ingramcontent.com/pod-product-compliance
Lightning Source LLC
Chambersburg PA
CBHW032050090426
42744CB00004B/151